INTERNATIONAL COUNCIL

ADULT CATECHESIS
IN THE
CHRISTIAN COMMUNITY

SOME PRINCIPLES AND GUIDELINES

ISBN 1-55586-402-3

TABLE OF CONTENTS

Part One
THE ADULTS TO WHOM CATECHESIS IS DIRECTED

Part Two
MOTIVATIONS, CRITERIA AND OTHER POINTS OF REFERENCE FOR ADULT CATECHESIS

Part Three
GUIDELINES FOR PRACTICAL IMPLEMENTATION

PRELIMINARY REMARKS

The International Council for Catechesis (COINCAT) took as the theme for its sixth plenary session, held in Rome October 23-29, 1988, the "Catechesis of Adults in the Christian Community".

The results of this session have been summarized in this document which, after being reviewed by the Congregation for the Clergy, of which COINCAT is a consultative body, is now being published under the sponsorship of COINCAT.

This document hopes to contribute to the efforts being made in the Christian communities spread throughout the world to promote adult catechesis, in keeping with the "new evangelization" so often called for by Pope John Paul II.

With this purpose in mind, the suggestions made here, in keeping with the most important pronouncements of the Magisterium on this question, reflect the expertise of members of the various local Churches throughout the world. This has allowed a great variety of approaches to emerge, but it has also permitted the identification of certain principles and features common to every form of adult catechesis.

This contribution does not intend to be an exhaustive directory for adult catechesis or a practical program ready for implementation. Rather, it simply offers some guidelines which, arranged in a systematic and organic way, reflect a rich world of experiences. These reflections are presented to pastoral workers and catechists in order to promote a deeper appreciation and implementation of adult catechesis.

In composing this document, the contributions of all the members of COINCAT were utilized, but the actual organization of the material and the writing of the text were the work of the Secretary General, who was assisted in this task by various experts.

May the Lord bless the service rendered by adult catechesis and grant His Church the grace to proclaim the Kingdom of God in ever more incisive ways through adult believers living in adult communities.

Easter 1990.

FR. CESARE BISSOLI, S.D.B.
Secretary General of COINCAT

ABBREVIATIONS

AG	Ad Gentes
CD	Christus Dominus
Chr.L.	Christifideles Laici
CT	Catechesi Tradendae
EN	Evangelii Nuntiandi
Gen.Cat.Dir.	General Catechetical Directory
LG	Lumen Gentium

INTRODUCTION

FROM THE PERSPECTIVE OF THE KINGDOM

1. "What comparison shall we use for the reign of God? What image will help to present it? It is like a mustard seed which, when planted in the soil, is the smallest of all the earth's seeds, yet once it is sown, springs up to become the largest of shrubs, with branches big enough for the birds of the sky to build nests in its shade" (*Mk* 4, 30-32).

This parable of Jesus sums up nicely for our time the dynamism of faith which is evident among people of all ages. In a particular way, through the proclamation of the Word, which in the beginning is humble and often arduous, adults receive the grace to become a living part of the Kingdom of God, are able to recognize their Lord and Saviour and become witnesses to Him among their brothers and sisters in the world.

This parable therefore captures succintly the *fundamental traits* of adult catechesis: its ultimate and radical purpose (the definitive coming of the Kingdom), the completely transcendent power which sustains it, the collaboration to which adults are necessarily called, and its extraordinarily positive impact on adults and on others.

2. Jesus said, "Only one is your Master and you are all brothers" (*Mt* 23, 8).

We recognize Jesus today as He was in His own time, as one who approaches every kind of person—women and men, the small and the great, the good and the evil, the poor and the rich—in order to proclaim the Good News of the Kingdom with truth, simplicity and love. In Him every adult finds the "Way, the Truth and the Life" (*Jn* 14, 6). The catechesis of adults, therefore, draws its own inspiration, courage and joy from the *Gospel of Jesus*.

3. The consciousness of just how complex the world is in which we live requires humility and realism on the part of pastoral workers and leads them to be ever attentive, in the proclamation of the Christian message, to the real conditions in which people live. This sensitivity helps to overcome the distance between Church and society, between faith and culture, which is an important issue in dealing with adults.

This means that adult catechesis, in pursuing its goals, must clearly discern the problems and expectations of people today and be alert to the positive elements in their situation which are emerging. With evangelical forthrightness, it must be able to show why the Kingdom of God announced by Jesus offers light and hope.

In the Footsteps of the Council

4. The *Magisterium of the Church,* imbued with the spirit of renewal of the Second Vatican Council (cf. *CD* 14; *AG* 14) has constantly affirmed with authority, clarity and insistence, the centrality and importance of the catechesis of adults.

John Paul II states that "one of the constant concerns whose urgency is confirmed by present day experience throughout the world, is the catechesis of adults. This is the principal form of catechesis because it is addressed to persons who have the greatest responsibility and the capacity to live the Christian message in its fully developed form" (*CT* 43).

5. It is certainly a gift of the Holy Spirit to witness in these years after the Council *the development of initiatives* on behalf of a new catechesis of adults in the local Churches throughout the world. This is manifested in pastoral letters, reflections and programs offered by experts and study centers, the implementation of the RCIA (the Rite of Christian Initiation of Adults) and a wide variety of other pastoral initiatives, all sustained by a truly ecclesial and missionary spirit.

In this spring of the catechesis of adults, the most notable developments in the various local Churches are the growth in the number of lay catechists, both women and men, and the fruitful and original activity of new groups, movements and associations.

In this context of hope, the same Spirit makes us all the more painfully aware of the limits and difficulties with which we are faced: the many adults who are not reached by any kind of catechesis, Christian communities lacking in missionary spirit, pastoral workers not sufficiently motivated by a sense of pastoral love and patience, an inadequate catechesis which too often is not integrated into a broader program of evangelization, and the lack in number and in preparation of catechists.

6. For this reason the Church makes a renewed call to all those most directly involved in the faith education of its members to increase their efforts to find *new ways* to reach those adults who have not been touched by the message of Christ, or who having been evangelized, have left the Church.

Responding to this call, the *International Council for Catechesis,* a consultative body of the Congregation for the Clergy, made a special study of adult catechesis during its 1988 session. As a result, the present document was elaborated, based on the experience of its members, clerical, religious, lay men and women, who come from various regions of the world and represent different races and cultures.

THE PURPOSE AND AUDIENCE OF THIS DOCUMENT

7. The present document intends to highlight only the most significant aspects of the catechesis of adults. It touches on *common issues,* common problems and probable solutions, which seem prevalent throughout the world, fully recognizing that inculturation will have to be made in the local Churches.

This document wishes therefore to stimulate a spirit of communion and solidarity with others, by encouraging the sharing of insights and resources necessary for carrying out the catechesis of adults.

8. This document is addressed to the whole People of God, gathered in the diverse Christian communities throughout the world, under the guidance of their Pastors.

In a more direct way it has in mind those *lay catechists* who are already engaged in the catechesis of adults or who are preparing themselves for this service.

They are living proof of the action of the Spirit who in every community continues to call forth people who make themselves available to accompany their brothers and sisters on their faith journey.

9. Certain elements in the Gospel Parable of the Sower provide a fitting way for articulating the three parts of this document:

— the "different kinds of terrain" on which the seed falls, i.e. the present situation and the signs of the presence and growth of adults in today's Church;

— the "seed" of the Word which is communicated by means of the catechesis of adults, together with the profound reasons which motivate its communication and the principles which govern it;

— the process of "sowing and reaping", in which some guidelines are offered for concrete action.

PART ONE

THE ADULTS TO WHOM CATECHESIS IS DIRECTED

10. To become an adult and to live as an adult is a vocation given by God to human beings, as illustrated in the very first pages of the Bible (cf. *Gen* 1, 27-28; 2, 15). This vocation finds its most perfect model in Jesus of Nazareth who "was almost thirty when He began His ministry" (*Lk* 3, 23) of proclaiming the Kingdom. To grow into and draw near to Him, the Perfect Man (cf. *Eph* 4, 13-15) becomes accordingly a grace and a task for every creature.

But how does this actually take place? What "lights" and "shadows", in the world and in the Church, characterize the human and Christian growth of adults?

IN THE WORLD

11. Our attention is drawn right away to the *difficulties and sufferings* which weigh heavily on so many adults, including Christians, both men and women. Among these we would like to single out the insufficient and disproportionate means for self-development (humanization); lack of respect for the basic rights to freedom, "among which religious freedom occupies a place of primary importance" (*EN* 39), as well as the right to follow one's own conscience and the right to personal dignity, especially with respect to the poor; and the obstacles to carrying out one's responsibilities to society and the family.

The causes of these evils are multiple and complex, and from time to time must be investigated. Generally speaking, we can point to the enormous disproportion in the distribution of the world's goods, the diminished regard for the family, the insufficient appreciation of women, lack of work, racial discrimination, the lack of access to culture, the incapacity or impossibility on the part of the masses to participate in public decision making.

These distortions gravely deform the image of God which men and women, precisely as adults, are called to reflect and fully enjoy (*Gen* 1, 26-27).

12. At the same time, we are witnessing an awakening of the individual and collective consciousness with respect to personal dignity, mutual interde-

pendence and communion, and the need to stand in solidarity with the weak and the poor.

Furthermore, respect for and interest in religion and spiritual values are on the rise among adults, who regard religion as a source from which their lives draw new strength. The awareness that the earth is a gift from God, which must be respected and protected from all forms of pollution, is also gaining ground.

Civil institutions, for their part, have in some places made a serious attempt to protect the rights and the freedom of individuals. They help adults to carry out their responsibilities through programs of continuing education, which extend up through old age.

IN THE CHURCH

13. The Church, which lives in the midst of the human family and is engaged like its Founder in the service of people, contributes to humanity by *proclaiming the Good News* of the Kingdom of God in Jesus the Saviour. In bringing about an ever more just and more fraternal human family, the Good News proclaimed by Jesus is indispensable.

Faithful to this task, the Church, which is always open to the contributions of human experience and science, regards adult catechesis as the path to follow as a disciple of Christ, a path which is incarnate in the concrete situations of life.

Thus, it is necessary at the start to recognize the various conditionings and challenges in the ecclesial communities which have the greatest influence on the growth of adults as Christians.

CONDITIONINGS AND CHALLENGES

14. "Why have you been standing here idle all day?" asked the Lord of the vineyard to the men who had been standing around all day. "No one has hired us," they told him. He answered them, "You go to the vineyard too" (*Mt* 20, 6-7).

In the parable of Jesus, which expresses the universal invitation to the Kingdom of God, we recognize the positive response of many, but we cannot overlook those—and they are the majority—who have not heard the invitation, or have forgotten it, or for various reasons cannot come to terms with it.

This is the actual situation, full of both serious drawbacks and positive opportunities, of accomplishments and expectations, which the Church has to take into account when proposing the Gospel to adults.

15.   On the *economic-social level,* large numbers of believers do not have access to religious formation through catechesis because of a relentless underdevelopment which, in fact, prevents the poor from being evangelized (*Lk* 4, 18), though this is their sacred right.

One could add here the migrations of whole peoples going on at present. Uprooted and displaced from their homelands, they are deprived of the basic need of security and stability.

16.   On the *social-cultural level,* in light of the determining influence of culture in all its various expressions, a number of important factors which have a decisive impact should be noted:

a) With the growth and expansion of the process of *secularization,* the very possibility of catechesis is put in crisis, particularly among adults, because of the great changes in culture and customs which have had significant repercussions, at least in the recent past, on the organization of life and the availability of time.

Much has also been said about the spiritual difficulties which adults have to face, such as the absence of human and religious certitudes, the loss of individual and collective identity, and the burden of loneliness.

b) Adults who are fervent in their faith sometimes find themselves in countries where the number of believers is small and resources are lacking, and where, on the other hand, *other great religions or value systems* exercise the predominant influence, which is not infrequently hostile to Christians.   Under these circumstances, catechesis encounters great difficulties in reconciling an authentic and original faith journey with the legitimate local culture.

It should also be remembered that in certain countries, because of the reigning ideology, religious gatherings are forbidden or prevented and pastoral and catechetical services in public places are seriously obstructed.

c) Everywhere, *technological development* applied to the problems of life and exacerbated beyond all bounds by the media, poses new problems, particularly for adults, which the Christian faith must address.

This challenge requires a new way of formulating and resolving the perennial problems, such as the meaning and value of life, the destiny of human beings and the world, living together with others, the relationship between faith and the moral life, and the primacy of religious and spiritual values.

17.   On the *level of the ecclesial communities,* it would be an oversight not to acknowledge the vigor of the Gospel seed in the realization of adult catechesis in the context of parishes, families, movements and groups, and in many other situations which will be discussed in Part Three.

Indeed, in taking to heart the invitation of Jesus, "Open your eyes and see! The fields are shining for harvest!" (*Jn* 4, 35), our attention is focussed on what it is possible to accomplish in the catechesis of adults.

There are, in fact, a number of identifiable needs which require a new approach in adult catechesis. These needs can only be met within the context of an adult Christian community.

There is a great need for:

a) a more adequate language of faith, which will be comprehensible to adults at all levels, from those who are illiterate or quasi-literate to those who are highly educated; unless this language is addressed to them, they will feel alienated from the Church and perceive catechesis as irrelevant;

b) more accessible places where un-churched adults will feel welcomed, and where adults who have gone through their catechumenate or some other form of initiation can continue their faith journey in a Christian community;

c) a wider variety of catechetical models responding to the local and cultural needs of the people;

d) the popular religiosity of the people, both in its content and expression, to be taken seriously; the aspects which reflect the Gospel should be prudently incorporated in catechesis;

e) a more consistent effort to reach out to all adults, especially those who are un-churched, alienated or marginated, responding to their needs, so as to counteract the widespread proselytizing by sects;

f) a more visible expression of sensitivity, availability and openness on the part of clergy and Church institutions toward adults, their problems and their need for catechesis.

18. By way of conclusion to this analysis and with a view to what follows, we can group the adults who need catechesis into the following categories, keeping in mind *Catechesi Tradendae* 44:

— adults in places which have become dechristianized, who have not been able to deepen their knowledge of the Gospel message;

— adults who were catechized beginning in childhood, but who have fallen away from the faith;

— adults who have benefited little from catechesis, either because they assorbed little or were incorrectly catechized;

— adults who were baptized as children but were not subsequently catechized, and who find themselves as adults, to a certain extent, in the situation of catechumens.

PART TWO

MOTIVATIONS, CRITERIA AND OTHER POINTS OF REFERENCE FOR ADULT CATECHESIS

19. "If one of you decides to build a tower, will he not first sit down and calculate the outlay to see if he has enough money to complete the project?" (*Lk* 14, 28).

In the exhortation of the Master to acquire the evangelical wisdom needed for every undertaking on behalf of the Kingdom of God, we are invited to recognize and state the fundamental reasons for adult catechesis in the Church, all the more so as its importance becomes recognized.

MOTIVATIONS

20. Theological-pastoral reflection proposes a number of different, complementary motives for catechesis: some in relationship to the faith life of the adult as such; others in relationship to the adult's public role in society and in ecclesial communities; and finally those which outrank the others in importance because they aim at the greater glory of God and the good of the Church.

21. Adults in the Church, that is, all Christians—men and women, lay people, priests and religious—are people who have a *right and an obligation to be catechized, just like everyone else* (*CT,* c. V; can. 217, 774; *Chr. L.* 34).

This reason does not derive from any kind of service which the adult Christian is called to render. It springs instead directly from the "seed" of faith planted within and which hopes to mature as the adult grows in age and responsibility. "When I was a child I used to talk like a child, think like a child, reason like a child. When I became a man I put childish ways aside" (*1 Cor* 13, 11).

Only by becoming an adult in the faith is one able to fulfill his or her adult duties toward others, as is required by the vocation given to each at baptism.

One must admit that in various communities, the formation of adults has been taken for granted or perhaps carried out in connection with certain events, not infrequently in an infantile way. Because certain external or traditional supports are sometimes lacking, a grave imbalance is created insofar as catechesis has devoted considerable attention to children while the same has not happened in the catechesis of young people and adults.

22. The need for personal formation is necessarily bound up with the role which adults assume in *public life*. They share with all Christians the task of witnessing to the Gospel in words and deeds, but they do this with undeniable authority and in a specifically adult way. This is true in the family context in which many adults, precisely as parents or other relatives, become both by nature and grace the first and indispensable catechists of their children. Adults also serve as role models for young people who need to be confronted with and challenged by the faith of adults.

In the context of society, the role of adults is crucial in the workplace and in the academic, professional, civil, economic, political and cultural spheres, and wherever responsibility and power are exercised. This is the case because the believing adult is so often the only one who can introduce the leaven of the Kingdom, express the novelty and beauty of the Gospel, and demonstrate the will for change and liberation desired by Jesus Christ.

The simple, faith-filled actions by which adults give witness to the Gospel in these situations require a great effort on their part to inwardly appropriate what they are called to pass on to others in a convincing and credible way.

23. This missionary task assumes greater weight in the context of the Christian community, which is called to acquire an adult faith.

It will be helpful to recall that this necessarily involves the intelligent and harmonious collaboration of all those who make up the Church, from children and young people to adults and the elderly.

In this context of communion, adults are asked in a special way to commit themselves to the *catechetical service and, in a broader sense, the pastoral care* of their brothers and sisters, both the little ones and grown-ups, always keeping in mind the different situations, problems and difficulties with which they are confronted.

It is not difficult to imagine what level of competence—and hence of previous formation—is required of adults in such a complex world, which is at one and the same time open to and wary of the Gospel of Jesus Christ.

24. A number of other motivations of a socio-religious, psychological and pedagogical-pastoral nature could be added. But all motivations converge on the most eminent and radical reason which is the basis of their validity and

meaning. This is the reason which derives from *the order of faith:* the glory of God, the building of the Kingdom and the good of the Church. Indeed, God is fittingly honoured by the person who is fully alive, and all the more so if the person is a mature adult. The Kingdom of God, like the seed in the field, grows above all through the activity of its adult members.

The Church herself, as well as every form of catechesis, are enriched by the charism of maturity and wisdom which comes from adults, and in this way the Church is helped in the effort of understanding the truth which is in gestation among the People of God.

A great number of adults, women and men, have offered a brilliant example of the contribution adults make when they collaborate with God in shaping the history of salvation, both in the constitutive period of the Bible and in the time of the Church, which actualizes Christ's salvation in her life.

25. In summary, in order for the Good News of the Kingdom to penetrate all the various layers of the human family, it is crucial that every Christian play an active part in the coming of the Kingdom. The work of each will be coordinated with and complementary to the contribution of everyone else, according to the different degrees of responsibility each one has. All of this naturally requires adults to play a primary role. Hence, it is not only legitimate, but necessary, to acknowledge that a fully Christian community can exist only when a systematic catechesis of all its members takes place and when an effective and well-developed catechesis of adults is regarded as the *central task* in the catechetical enterprise.

BASIC CRITERIA

In light of the motivations which we have just set forth, it will be possible to identify some criteria which support an effective and valid catechesis of adults.

We will single out five particularly important criteria, whose application in practice will be taken up in Part Three.

26. A catechesis of adults will be acutely sensitive to *men and women insofar as they are adults.* It will approach them in their adult situation, which is for the most part the lay state, and will be attentive to their problems and experiences. It will make use of their spiritual and cultural resources, always respecting the differences among them. Finally, adult catechesis will stimulate the active collaboration of adults in the catechesis which involves them.

27.　This implies, as a second criterion, that the catechesis of adults is realized with full recognition and appreciation of the "secular character which is proper and peculiar to the laity", which qualifies them "to seek the Reign of God in temporal affairs, putting them into relationship with God" (*LG* 31).

In this regard, it is worth remembering what the Apostolic Exhortation *Evangelii Nuntiandi* and later, in the same words, *Christifideles Laici,* described as the responsibilities of the Christian laity: "Their own field of evangelizing activity is the vast and complicated world of politics, society and economics, as well as the world of culture, of the sciences and the arts, of international life, of the mass media.　It also includes other realities, which are open to evangelization, such as human love, the family, the education of children and adolescents, professional work, and suffering.　The more Gospel-inspired lay people there are engaged in these realities, clearly involved in them, competent to promote them and conscious that they must exercise to the full their Christian powers which are often repressed and buried, the more these realities will be at the service of the Kingdom of God and therefore at the service of salvation in Jesus Christ, without in any way losing or sacrificing their human content but rather pointing to a transcendent dimension which is often disregarded" (*EN* 70; *Chr. L.* 23).

28.　One of the most valid criteria in the process of adult catechesis, but which is often overlooked, is the *involvement of the community* which welcomes and sustains adults.　Adults do not grow in faith primarily by learning concepts, but by sharing the life of the Christian community, of which adults are members who both give and receive from the community.

29.　The catechesis of adults, therefore, can bear fruit only *within the overall pastoral plan* of the local Church communities.　It must have its own distinctive place in the whole, since it aims at making adults constructive participants in the life and mission of the community.

This implies two fundamental principles operative in all forms of adult catechesis:

— Even considering the autonomy of the process of adult catechesis, we must keep in mind that it must be integrated with liturgical formation and formation in Christian service.

— Adult catechesis cannot be conducted to the exclusion or slighting of catechesis for other age groups.　When coordinated with them, it becomes the catechesis of Christian maturity and the goal of other kinds of catechesis.

By reason of its special position and the contribution it makes to the growth of the whole community's faith journey, the catechesis of adults must be regarded as a preferential option.

30.   Finally, following the example of Jesus, who taught the people "the message in a way they could understand" (*Mk* 4, 33), the catechesis of adults must recall in a particular way the responsibility of the local Churches, on the one hand, to remain united with the whole People of God, on the basis of the unique Gospel message authentically proclaimed in all its integrity and, on the other hand, to reflect on their own local situations in order to adapt the presentation of the message of salvation to the needs of the people.

The wisdom that is the fruit of experience, prayer and study will guide catechists to maintain a balance between making all the necessary *adaptations* and *being faithful* to what constitutes the common heritage of catechesis.

Points of Reference

31.   Attempting to define adulthood in an univocal way is quite complex, given the number of factors at play in different, complementary interpretations.   The contributions of the psychological, social and pedagogical sciences must all be carefully considered, although always directly in rapport with the specific life context, in which the ethnic, cultural and religious factors peculiar to that environment play a significant role.

Particularly today, it is essential to keep in mind the relationship between the young generation and that of adults, since the two groups influence and condition each other in a wide variety of ways.

To respect the "mystery of adulthood" and to organize well all forms of pastoral service for adults means keeping in mind all these factors and the very diverse ways of speaking about and being an adult.

32.   It is not at all easy, from a practical viewpoint, to provide a precise and uniform definition of the *catechesis of adults.* The reasons and criteria for its significance and necessity have already been pointed out.   There are differences over the best way to put adult catechesis into practice, with respect to the scope of the subject matter, the length of time needed, and the most suitable arrangement of the material for a given audience.

Here, in light of recent Church documents, we understand catechesis as one moment in the total process of evangelization (*EN* 17; *CT* 18).

The specific role of the catechesis of adults consists in an initial deepening of the faith received at baptism, in an elementary, complete and systematic way (*CT* 21), with a view to helping individuals all life long grow to the full maturity of Christ (cf. *Eph* 4, 13).

Catechesis *per se* has to be *distinguished* therefore from other activities, even though it cannot be separated from them:

— it is different from evangelization, which is the proclamation of the Gospel for the first time to those who have not heard it, or the re-evangelization of those who have forgotten it;

— it is different from formal religious education, which goes beyond the basic elements of faith in more systematic and specialized courses;

— it is also different from those informal occasions for faith awareness in God's presence, which arise in fragmentary and incidental ways in the daily life of adults.

At the same time, adult catechesis remains *closely related* to all the above aspects of faith development:

— it makes explicit in the life of adults the reality of God's message (kerygma), taking into consideration concrete human situations, and "translating" it into the cultural language of the people;

— it goes to the core of the doctrinal content of our Catholic faith, presenting the fundamental beliefs of the creed in a way that relates to the life experience of people, instilling in them a faith mentality;

— it calls for a structured and organized, though perhaps very elementary, faith journey, which is expressed and sustained by listening to the Word of God, by celebration (liturgy), by charitable service (diakonia), and by a forthright witness in the various situations in which adults find themselves.

PART THREE

GUIDELINES FOR PRACTICAL IMPLEMENTATION

33. The common operative features of adult catechesis are presented here according to the four most important areas:

— the qualities of the adult Christian, which constitute the objective of catechesis and determine its content as well as certain constant factors in the way it is presented;

— the process involved in adult catechesis, with special reference to its methodological principles, forms and models;

— catechists of adults and their formation;

— those responsible for adult catechesis in the community.

QUALITIES OF THE CHRISTIAN ADULT IN THE FAITH

34. St. Paul admonishes the Christians of Ephesus in a fatherly way "to be children no longer, tossed here and there". As he goes on to explain, this is because it is our vocation to become the "perfect man," worthy of the infinite riches of Christ, who fills the universe (cf. *Eph* 4, 13-14; 1, 23; 3, 8).

The ultimate and unifying goal of adult catechesis is to help the mature Christian to live as an adult by acquiring certain qualities. These qualities can be grouped around three major goals, which are in turn rooted in a common vision and then articulated in certain objectives and specified in content.

a) *Goals*

35. Everywhere in the Church, the need to build *adult Christian communities* has been noticed. These communities must express a clear faith identity and must be centered on a clear proclamation of the Gospel, a meaningful celebration of the liturgy and a courageous witness in charity.

All catechesis must be directed to this goal, beginning with the catechesis of little children. Obviously, in the catechesis of adults the effects are more immediate and incisive.

Only in this way can we create convincing signs and effective conditions for an adherence to the faith which is stable and fruitful.

36. "The Reign of God is at hand. Reform your lives and believe in the Gospel!" (*Mk* 1, 15).

These words of Jesus establish the first and enduring goal of anyone who wishes to be one of his mature disciples: to acquire an attitude of *conversion to the Lord.*

The catechesis of adults promotes an openness of the heart to the mystery of the Lord's greatness and grace by encouraging sincere reconciliation with the Lord and with one's brothers and sisters. Adults are led to recognize and accept the Lord's call and His salvific plan by living a life which is pleasing to God and which aims at holiness (cfr. *Chr. L.* 16-17). Adult catechesis is an invitation to faithfully practice the discipleship of Jesus and to judge all personal, social and spiritual experiences in the light of faith.

37. "They devoted themselves to the apostles' instruction and the communal life, to the breaking of bread and the prayers" (*Acts* 2, 42).

The conversion to the Lord at baptism leads to membership in a community whose way of life as disciples of Christ is shared by all. The catechesis of adults aims at bringing to fruition a conscious and firm decision to live the gift and choice of faith through *membership in the Christian community.* Adults who are mature in the faith understand what it means to be in communion with others and accept their coresponsibility for the community's mission and internal life.

38. "You are the salt of the earth... You are the light of the world. In the same way, your light must shine before men so that they may see goodness in your acts and give praise to your heavenly father" (*Mt* 5, 13-16).

Recognizing the strong commitment to the new evangelization to which the Spirit is calling the Church today everywhere in the world, adult catechesis gives a missionary purpose to those tasks for which it is responsible.

Adult catechesis makes one more willing and able to be a *Christian disciple in the world* in that it helps to differentiate between good and evil, especially in the most significant expressions of one's culture, and to recognize and accept "all that is true, all that deserves respect, all that is honest, pure, admirable, decent, virtuous, or worthy of praise" (*Phil* 4, 8). Adult catechesis also draws others into one's faith-working-in-love (*Gal* 5, 6), and provides reasons for the hope that one has (*1 Pet* 3, 15). It knows how to come to terms with the longings for liberation and salvation of people in every age, especially the poor, and then it takes effective steps in favor of the transformation of family, social and professional life in the light of the Gospel.

In this way, a harmonious and vital synthesis of the essential characteristics of the Christian, appropriate for adults, is being brought about. These characteristics are an obedient listening to the Word of God, communion with the faith community, and the service of charity and witness in the world.

b) *Objectives*

The goals which have been mentioned can be attained through *objectives* which specify more concretely the catechetical journey.

Recalling that the catechetical apostolate aims at active participation in the life and mission of the Church, including direct participation in the pastoral programs of the Church, we propose the following objectives to be of particular relevance and universal application.

39.   A *basic understanding of the Church's faith, presented in a sufficiently organic way together with the reasons for believing.* It should be drawn directly from the sources of Revelation; that is, the Bible, the Liturgy, the Fathers, the Magisterium of the Church, other great documents of the Tradition, and the experience of Christian living in the ecclesial communities.

40.   *An appropriate assimilation of the theological and cultural heritage in which faith is expressed.* This implies a knowledge of the major religious signs and symbols of faith, the role and use of the Bible, a grasp of the significance and practice of liturgical and private prayer, and an awareness of the impact of religious belief on culture and its institutions.

41.   The capacity of *Christian discernment* in various situations, particularly regarding ethical principles which bear on human life and dignity and which have to do with respect for justice and the cause of the weak and the poor. Always in a spirit of respect for others, one also needs to develop a critical sense in the face of other religions or ways of life which people find meaningful.

42.   Finally, the acquisition of those *skills and abilities which allow the adult believer to carry out his Christian witness* in the most diverse circumstances, in the community and in society.

c) *Contents*

The contents of adult catechesis must be as comprehensive and exhaustive as possible. It is important to adapt the didactic methodology employed to the situations and needs of any given audience. Corresponding to the objectives indicated and the major common needs of adult believers today, these are the basic components of adult catechesis:

43. Catechesis has to present in a comprehensive and systematic way the *great themes of the Christian religion* which involve faith and reasons for believing: the mystery of God and the Trinity, Christ, the Church, the sacraments, human life and ethical principles, eschatological realities, and other contemporary themes in religion and morality. It will respect the hierarchy of truths and their interrelationship.

44. In the context of a more than ever complex and pluralistic society, particular importance will be attached to a knowledge of the truths of the Gospel, and to the Church's duty to enlighten and educate the moral conscience. Catechesis presents the *ethical implications* of the Christian vision for major problems which emerge in personal and collective situations, such as the dignity of every person, the inviolable right to life, the transmission and protection of human life, the promotion of social justice, solidarity and peace, as well as concern for the poor, the powerless and the forgotten (*Chr. L.* 37-41).

45. Catechesis must lead to a knowledge and evaluation, in the light of faith, of the *socio-cultural order* and of the changes that are taking place in the world today and in the life of individuals, affirming what is good but also pointing out what is harmful and contrary to the Gospel. It has to clarify the distinction between action in the temporal order and in the ecclesial order, between political commitment and the commitment to evangelization, while drawing attention to the various ways they can influence one another (*Gen. Cat. Dir.* 97; *Chr. L.* 42-43).

46. To help bring adults to completeness and full maturity in their knowledge of the Christian faith, catechesis must include an *introduction* to the reading and use of Sacred Scripture, both private and communal, as well as the most important expressions of liturgy and prayer. It would also be most useful if catechesis presented the major moments in the history of the Church, both universal and local, as well as the principal documents of the Church's Magisterium, especially regarding social doctrine.

d) Constant Elements in the Presentation of Content

47. "All the people made a great feast for they had understood the meaning of the words they heard" (*Neh* 8, 12). These words describe the joy the people experienced when, after returning from exile, they were able to understand the Scriptures. Later, Jesus and the apostles imparted their message in an exemplary way so that the people could understand (*Mk* 4, 33; *1 Cor* 14, 19). Hence, we should consider it the Lord's will that in teaching the faith, we present it in a readily understandable way.

The contents of adult catechesis are offered to men and women of every social and cultural background as the nourishing and satisfying bread of life so that, filled with divine wisdom, they might radiate this wisdom in all areas of life.

These considerations allow us to identify certain principles which govern the presentation of content and which concretize the basic criteria enunciated above (nn. 26-30).

48. In the presentation of the Christian religion, catechesis must deal with the many *questions,* difficulties and doubts which arise in the human heart. Indeed, these questions should be brought to light when they have been obscured or confused by ignorance or indifference. The faith response to these questions will appear meaningful if it is rooted in the Bible and in concrete historical life, and if it is respectful of reason and attentive to the signs of the times.

49. Precisely because the principal content of adult catechesis is the revelation of the living God who saves human beings and helps them to realize their full potential, this catechesis must be dynamic and relevant so that adults, to their own satisfaction, can become gradually more aware of *their value and dignity as human beings,* as a result of a careful and stimulating exposition of the great truths of faith.

50. Conscious of how secularized and pluralistic the world of the adult can be, the catechesis of adults seeks to provide solid formation *in a spirituality suitable for the Christian laity* (cf. n. 27). The special tasks of the Christian lay person in the Church and in society, which vary according to the widely different situations in which adults find themselves, should be given a prominent place in the formation program. Special attention should be reserved for teaching adults how to pray.

51. Catechesis of adults must encourage *an ecumenical outlook* (*CT* 32-34). It must be open to *confronting and entering into dialogue* with the great religions and

with those attitudes, theories and practices which constantly seek to attract adults. "The catechesis of adults will be surer of success when it is open to the encounter between faith, culture and science, in which an attempt is made to integrate them with one another while respecting the specific identity of each" (John Paul II, Discourse to the members of COINCAT, in *L'Osservatore Romano*, 30 Oct. 1988, p. 4).

Hence, whatever knowledge and methodologies allow a more adequate reading of historical, social and religious phenomena, both in their negative and positive aspects, have a right to a place in adult catechesis. With their help, catechesis will be able to provide a more enlightened Christian interpretation of reality.

52. Since the constructive contribution of adults in giving witness to their faith in the family and in many other areas of life is clearly recognized, catechesis must help adults to learn not only for themselves, but should prepare them to *communicate the contents of faith to others*. They can make an important contribution in showing other adults what an impact the faith can have on their lives and on the world around them. In a particular way, they have a responsibility for the disadvantaged, especially the poor and marginated, and all who find themselves in especially trying circumstances.

53. Finally, as an underpinning for the needs just mentioned, the *communitarian dimension* of the contents of faith will be thoroughly developed. In this way, adults will come to know and experience the "mystery of the Church", which is incarnate in a particular community and history and which is characterized by particular needs, initiatives and pace of life. Catechesis will help adults see how they can fit in and participate in the life of the Church.

METHODOLOGICAL CONSIDERATIONS

54. The widely varying kinds of adults and life circumstances which adult catechesis must take into consideration make it impossible to provide a catalogue of fixed norms applicable to every program of adult catechesis. Nevertheless, the results of our reflection on adult catechesis permit us to identify several reference points which are valid for all situations. These common features apply to the recipients of catechesis, organizational principles, and the forms and models of catechesis.

a) *The Recipients of Catechesis*

We have repeatedly stressed that the adult formation process has its own particular characteristics. A central feature is the establishment of a friendly and dialogical rapport. This means that the didactic moment must be integrated into a broader and more elaborate faith journey, of which we would like to point out a number of aspects.

55. There are certain *special categories* which deserve attention because of their intrinsic value, both from a merely human as well as an evangelical perspective. Here we have in mind those whose need for the consolation of the Christian message is all the greater because of the intensity of their isolation and suffering. These include the disabled, the elderly, the sick, and all who find themselves on the fringes of society (refugees, immigrants, nomads and prisoners). The possibility of their involvement in the Christian community is often underestimated and unappreciated. With the solicitude of Christ, catechesis will also show special concern for those living in irregular situations.

56. Above all, one must begin by *accepting adults where they are.* To make more explicit what was said in n. 26, it is essential to keep in mind the specific adults with whom one is working, their cultural background, human and religious needs, their expectations, faith experiences, and their potential. It is also important to be attentive to their marital and professional status.

Individual groups should be as homogeneous as possible so that their participants will benefit from their experience.

57. Of fundamental importance is the *dialogical approach* which, while recognizing that all are called to the obedience of faith (*Rm* 1, 5), respects the basic freedom and autonomy of adults and encourages them to engage in an open and cordial dialogue. In this way, they can make known their needs and can participate, as they should, as subjects or agents in their own catechesis and in that of others.

58. On a more practical level, to maintain a good relationship with adults, their catechesis must include a clear witness to the Christian life and must focus on the essential issues, as it seeks to express itself in a solid and convincing way. Moreover, the truths of faith should be presented as certitudes, without taking away from the fact that for pilgrims on their way toward the full revelation of truth and life, the path of research and investigation always remains open.

b) *Organizational Principles*

59.   Practically speaking, under the term "adult catechesis" a variety of programs can be grouped.   Some are traditional; others are new.   They can be structured or more spontaneous, permanent or temporary, widely used or restricted in number and frequency.

One often has the impression that there is a wealth of initiatives, which however are wasteful of resources and badly organized, and do not match the sort of catechesis outlined so far.

To guarantee an effective catechetical program, the interaction of a number of factors, assisted by God's grace, is necessary: a good pastoral plan, the participation of the Christian community, the creation of positive experiences.

Moreover, in order for this interaction to work, catechesis must have an organic development and cannot be merely episodic.   To this end, every program or journey must be *systematic and organic,* and structured around precise goals.   It must ensure continuity in regularly scheduled meetings and must be clear about what is to be accomplished, even in only occasional or one-time programs.

In order to ensure unity in faith and life, when there are a number of different catechetical programs within the same community, all the programs need to contain certain common elements; namely, communion centered on the Word, participation in the liturgy, charitable service, and attentiveness to the Church's life.

60.   Certain *forms* of adult catechesis seem particularly suitable because of the impact they have and should therefore not be neglected.   Among these are programs aimed at families (parents, couples ...), student groups, parish organizations or other associations, and groups which gather on the occasion of a significant event (preparation for the sacraments, funerals, community celebrations, popular feast days, etc.).

61.   The *parish* has "the essential task of a more personal and immediate formation of the lay faithful" (*Chr. L.* 61).

Since it is in a position to reach out to individual persons and groups, it is the "privileged place" where "catechesis is realized not only through formal instruction, but also in the liturgy, sacraments and charitable activity" (John Paul II, Discourse to the members of COINCAT; cf. *Chr. L.* 26-27; 61).   Catechesis allows adults to have "a more direct and concrete perception of the sense of ecclesial communion and responsibility in the Church's mission" (*Chr. L.* 61).

A typical pattern for adult catechesis is the structuring of programs in certain clearly defined periods of time, particularly during the important seasons of Advent and Lent. In this way, catechesis recognizes the true value of the liturgical year, which is an important element in the Church's educational process.

62. In various places, *small communities* of adults (basic Christian communities) have emerged. Here the members carry out catechesis through praying and reflecting together on the Word of God. They strive to discover the relevance of the Word for their everyday life and particularly for their society, to whose service they have lovingly and generously dedicated themselves.

Organized by good leaders who are in harmony with the local Church, these communities can be a powerful and effective way by which adults can bring the Gospel to the world, as the leaven of holiness and liberation.

63. As for the kinds of catechesis carried out by the *various movements and associations,* a plurality of approaches is legitimate. Their programs offer "... the possibility, each with its own method, of offering a formation through a deeply shared experience in the apostolic life ..." (*Chr. L.* 62). Yet no movement should consider itself the only valid one and, above all, none should forget the principles of ecclesial communion (*Chr. L.* 30). As an act of the Church, catechesis must everywhere express the fullness of the Christian faith and should be in the service of ecclesial communion. It is important to keep in mind the great majority of the People of God who do not belong to any movement.

In light of the tremendous spiritual and apostolic impact which the movements have had, it is appropriate to inform adults about them and encourage their participation.

64. Undoubtedly a useful instrument for imparting a knowledge of the faith and for maintaining communion in the faith are *adult catechisms,* approved by the proper ecclesiastical authority (cf. can. 775, §§ 1-2). In conjunction with them, the resources of the sciences of communications and language should be utilized in order to communicate the Christian message with greater facility and effectiveness. We can never recall too often that "the language used must elicit the attention and interest of modern adults. The best forms of communication for reaching them, including signs, gestures and symbols, must be employed" (John Paul II, Discourse to the members of COINCAT).

65. The *mass media,* when used skillfully, are effective means of adult catechesis. The most prominent means of social communication are the press, radio and television, but videotapes, audiotapes, films, comic books, and other forms of the "minimedia" are also useful.

Professional Catholic lay people should be encouraged by all means to serve in news agencies and production centers, especially when these belong to the Church. They should strive to produce high quality resource materials.

c) *Models and Itineraries*

In recent times, various models have been proposed for adult catechesis, some of which transcend parish boundaries and may even have an international character. It has been said that the various itineraries are tailored to the spiritual condition of adults.

To assist the implementation of the various models, some clarifications and suggestions are in order.

66. The Synod of 1977 affirmed that "the model of all catechesis" is the catechumenate which culminates in baptism (*Synod Message* 8; cf. *EN* 44; *Chr. L.* 61). According to ancient tradition, every form of catechesis should be inspired by the catechumenal model. Precisely because the catechesis of adults aims at living the Christian life in all its fullness and integrity, the process outlined in the *catechumenate* seems the most appropriate model and should be encouraged everywhere, though it cannot be considered the exclusive model.

67. In the Church, the classic *catechumenal model* consists in a number of stages (cf. RCIA). The three which are considered most important are:

— the pre-catechumenate, which concentrates on the conversion of adults by presenting them with the kerygma or first proclamation of the Gospel;

— the catechumenate which forms adults in the basic components of the Catholic faith, summed up in the Creed, the liturgical celebration, and Christian living;

— the mystagogy, through which the neophytes deepen their knowledge of Christian doctrine and build on the basic catechesis already received.

68. The decision as to *which itineraries* are to be taken will depend on the situation in which adults find themselves. As already pointed out in Part One (n. 18), some need pre-evangelization to stimulate an interest in the faith. Others are ready for evangelization, the "kerygmatic moment" in which the Gospel is proclaimed. Finally, those who are farthest along are ready for catechesis in the strict sense.

In pastoral planning, the specific itinerary needed for a particular group of adults must be identified and the specifically catechetical dimension in programs for adults should be respected.

69. Adult catechesis necessarily aims at making the adult a member of and a participant in the community. This means that adults must not only know the community, but must also actively participate in its various faith expressions and accept some form of responsibility for community life. For this reason, the building of *small communities or ecclesial groups* is conducive to the strengthening of adult catechesis (cf. *CT* 24).

The Identity and Formation of the Catechist of Adults

70. "The harvest is good but laborers are scarce. Beg the harvest master to send out laborers to gather the harvest" (*Mt* 9, 37-38).

The harvest is the seed of the Kingdom which has grown to maturity, that is, the crowds which, though "prostrate from exhaustion", are eager for a shepherd who will take pity on them (*Mt* 9, 35-36; *Mk* 6, 34). Jesus says that generous harvesters are needed.

In the light of faith, we can see a marvelous response to this invitation at work in the Church today in the emergence of a large number of *catechists,* particularly from among the laity. They are involved with every age group, including the often challenging category of adults.

The requirements of adult catechesis described above highlight the decisive role of catechists as well as the qualities they must possess. "Forming those who, in turn, will be given the responsibility for the formation of the lay faithful, constitutes a basic requirement of assuring the general and widespread formation of all the lay faithful" (*Chr. L.* 63).

a) *Fundamental Requirements*

71. In general, the catechist of adults, whether a priest, religious or lay person, must have an *adult faith* and be capable of supporting and leading other adults on their journey of growth in the faith. If a catechist is not a natural leader, it will be necessary for him or her to acquire certain basic leadership skills.

Catechists do not regard themselves as superior or extrinsic to the persons or groups to whom they minister. Rather, in the process of growing in the faith, they feel one with and indebted to everyone, and they know how to recognize everyone and make them agents and participants in the faith journey.

72. Stability and living the Christian faith as a member of the ecclesial community are basic requirements for catechists. They must mature as spiritual persons in the concrete tasks they perform, in such a way that the "first word"

they speak is that of personal witness. To this must be added a professional competence, or the ability to sustain a catechetical journey with their brothers and sisters.

73. More precisely, an indispensable quality of catechists is the wise insight which allows them to go beyond the interpretation of texts to a deep grasp of vital issues and contemporary problems, and to be able to critically interpret present day events and the "signs of the times". Other requirements are the ability to listen and dialogue, encourage and reassure, form relationships, work in teams, and build community. There must also be a sense of being sent by the Church and of being accepted by the community, whose journey they share in a fraternal spirit.

In a word, the catechist of adults will be a sufficiently balanced human being, with the flexibility to adapt to different circumstances.

b) *Plurality in the Types of Catechists*

74. Room should be made for a *plurality of types* among adult catechists, in relationship to the needs of the community and according to the Spirit which each receives. There is a primary need for catechists who know how to work with families, persons or groups with particular needs, such as the disabled, the poor, the marginated, and those in irregular situations.

75. A true sign of God's love in our time is the emergence of *lay catechists of adults,* whose growth in number and competence we have identified as one of the most reassuring developments in the Church today (cf. n. 5). Precisely because of the charism of the lay state, they are in a better position than anyone else to accompany adults along their faith journey since they share the same tasks and problems in the family, society and the Church. They can also render a service which is essential in the catechesis of adults: the inculturation of the faith.

76. For all these reasons, the number of lay catechists—women and men, singles and married couples—will have to continue to grow since their number is not yet equal to the demand for them. At times, according to the need, they will require specialized training.

Always and in every way, lay catechists should be *recognized, respected and loved* by their priests and communities. They should be supported in their formation and encouraged and helped to accomplish a task which is indispensable but far from easy. Theirs is a genuine service through which God in Christ continues His work of mercy and salvation in the world.

c) *Formation*

77. More than ever we are aware that catechists, and particularly catechists of adults, are not born as such, but become catechists in two stages: *the initial formation program followed by continuing education.*

The development of a program must take into consideration the particular circumstances of the local Church, the people's needs, the catechists' skills and abilities, and the resources available. In a realistic, well thought out plan, there will be an initial formation program for future catechists, which lays the foundation for possible specialization. Later on, periodic updating will take place, in which instruction in theory will be supplemented by the insights of experience and a supervised apprenticeship.

78. Since the primary purpose of formation is growth in the faith, the core of the catechists' formation will be identical with that of the adult Christian. This includes a solid theological, anthropological and cultural preparation, carried out with the catechetical mission in mind and, hence, with particular attention to didactic-pedagogical questions.

79. Especially for the lay catechist, formation will be at one and the same time theoretical and practical, intellectual and spiritual. It will insist on the development of interpersonal relationships and a community-oriented attitude, always keeping in mind methods suitable for adult formation. Only in this way can the secular character of the lay catechist's identity and mission be expressed.

80. The formation of catechists must be responsibly directed by the local Church, under the guidance of the bishop and the appropriate offices, commissions and institutes of formation, in accordance with approved principles and programs.

One can be recognized as an adult catechist only after the required introductory formation program, as approved by the local Church, and after receiving a mandate from the bishop.

THOSE RESPONSIBLE FOR CATECHESIS IN THE COMMUNITY

81. The catechesis of adults, as a service of the Church on behalf of the Kingdom of God, is conceived and nurtured in the womb of Mother Church. For this reason, the *whole Christian community* should be involved in it, all the more so because adults determine the quality of Church life and guarantee its smooth operation. For this reason, adult catechesis should be carefully planned in the

parish, advertized in advance and supervised as it unfolds in its various stages. The community should pray for its success and joyfully offer its encouragement and support.

82.   Within the Christian community, the *bishop* as Teacher of the faith (cf. *CT* 63), is the chief catechist of adults.   He brings to this service the contribution of his own charism and personal witness.   He should take a keen interest in the diocesan program of adult catechesis and keep abreast of its activities through meetings with the moderators or directors and with the catechists themselves, whom he should treat as close collaborators.   The bishop should also devote care and attention to the formation of adult catechists.

Because of the responsibility he bears, the bishop will also follow, in a spirit of fraternal charity, the various forms of adult catechesis which do not originate within the diocese.

Because of the complexity and importance of adult catechesis, it is recommended that the bishop appoint at least one person to direct and coordinate the various initiatives on behalf of adult catechesis in the diocese.

It is only right to acknowledge that, in some countries, well-trained lay people serve as directors of adult catechesis on the diocesan and parish levels. Their contribution should be encouraged and supported.

83.   What the bishop assumes responsibility for on the diocesan level, *priests assume responsibility for in the local communities.* They should be directly involved in the catechesis of adults, and as directors of lay catechists, they should treat them with concern and respect.

Since the role of the priest in the community is irreplaceable, it is essential that *candidates for the priesthood have a solid formation in catechetics.*   This is particularly true with respect to adult catechesis, for which they need to learn to direct and collaborate with lay catechists.

84.   The present document, within the limits it has set for itself, may be a useful instrument for existing *national, regional and diocesan programs* in the various local Churches, which will naturally adapt the suggestions made here to their own pastoral circumstances.

This is also true for the various groups, movements and associations which offer catechesis for adults.   Through close association with the pastors of the Church, a true spirit of ecclesial communion can be created in the various forms of catechesis and so they will be sure that their apostolic endeavors are authentic and constructive.

CONCLUSION

85. Since there are many obstacles to adult catechesis in our times, there must be a willingness to accept even modest success and to exercise utmost *courage and patience* in the face of the failure of even the finest initiatives. Through repeated efforts and, above all, through an unshakeable faith in God, one is drawn into the Mystery of the Kingdom: a small seed which slowly but surely grows, for the joy and salvation of all.

86. In the light of all these reflections, it is fitting to turn our attention to the *Virgin Mary,* as she is repeatedly described in the Gospels as one who listens attentively and knows how to meditate in the depths of her heart (cf. *Lk* 1, 29; 2, 19.51; *Acts* 1, 14). We rightly see in Mary the exemplary model of the adult who undertakes the journey of faith. She listens to the Word of God and knows how to discover it in the complex events in which her life is caught up from the beginning. She listens, and as an adult person, she meditates at length; she searches within herself and seeks to understand the Will of God. Once she knows it, she generously accepts it and puts it into practice.

Later on, with utmost human sensitivity and a true missionary spirit, Mary knows how to interpret and respond to the questions of the various people she encounters, like those of the couple at the wedding feast of Cana. Through her, a catechist as much in deeds as in words, the grace of Christ could reach all these people.

May Mary of Nazareth, the faithful and courageous servant of God and of human beings, whom we see present as the Church begins her mission of evangelization and catechesis, inspire every adult who sets out on the journey of faith. At the same time, may she be the teacher and model of catechists who, like her, with their store of knowledge and wisdom, cheerfully put themselves at the service of their adult brothers and sisters.